$18.95

Aquariums

Jennifer B. Gillis

Rourke

Publishing LLC
Vero Beach, Florida 32964

www.rourkepublishing.com

PHOTO CREDITS: All photos © Lynn M. Stone

Editor: Robert Stengard-Olliges

Cover design by Michelle Moore.

imprint

Dedication: The publisher wishes to thank Jill Puckett, Educator, of the North Carolina State Aquarium, for her expertise in the preparation of this book.

Library of Congress Cataloging-in-Publication Data

Gillis, Jennifer Blizin, 1950-.
  Aquariums / Jennifer Blizin Gillis.
      p. cm. -- (Field trips)
  Includes index.
  ISBN 978-1-60044-558-3
  1. Aquariums, Public--Juvenile literature. I. Title.
  QL78.G57 2008
  597'.073--dc22

                                  2007017252

Printed in the USA

CG/CG

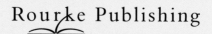

Rourke Publishing

www.rourkepublishing.com – rourke@rourkepublishing.com
Post Office Box 3328. Vero Beach. FL 32964

Table of Contents

Welcome to the Aquarium

Our rivers and oceans are alive with fish and other animals. The trouble is, without **scuba gear** we can see only a few of them. At an aquarium you can see animals that live in rivers, ponds, and oceans. Aquariums help people and scientists learn more about oceans and the animals that live in them.

▲
Aquariums are homes for aquatic
animals like this Snook.

Who Will You Meet?

An **educator** may take your class through the aquarium. You may see **aquarists** cleaning tanks or taking care of sea animals. You may see **technicians** cutting up food for the fish or making sure the water in the tanks is clean.

A aquarist checks a sea star in a tide pool exhibit. ▶

Freshwater and Saltwater

First, you may see some freshwater animals. The water in rivers and lakes is called freshwater. The insides of freshwater tanks look like the bottoms of lakes and rivers.

Then, you will see saltwater animals that live in the ocean. There are often many different tanks for saltwater animals. Each tank looks like a different part of the ocean.

This tank shows fish found in a mix of freshwater and saltwater (brackish water).

The Splash Zone

Walking on the beach at the edge of the ocean, you might find shells and parts of sea animals. This part of the ocean is called the splash zone. Aquariums often have a splash zone exhibit with live sea animals. You can touch them and learn about how they live, but clean your hands afterwards!

Please touch! Kids and adults enjoy sea creatures in tide pool exhibits. ▶

Coral Reefs

In parts of the world where the weather is warm, the ocean water looks clear and blue. Below the waves are **coral reefs**, where colorful fish swim. Real coral reefs are made of tiny animals. In the aquarium, the coral reefs are made of concrete. The beautiful fish and other sea animals are real, though.

▲

The tropical sea comes to life in an
aquarium's coral reef exhibit.

13

Deep Sea Creatures

Many kinds of fish live deep in the ocean. At the aquarium, the biggest tank is filled with these animals. You may see large sharks and sea turtles swimming around and around the tank. In the wild some of these fish might attack each other. In the aquarium they get fed every day, so they leave each other alone.

A diver prepares to enter a giant fish tank.▶

Feeding the Fish

In the aquarium, there is a special kitchen where aquarists make food for each kind of animal. The food has to be just the right size for the animal that eats it. Tiny sea animals, such as sea horses, eat brine shrimp. Larger sea animals eat different kinds of fish and squid. They also eat a kind of brown cube called gel food that is full of vitamins.

▲
A aquarist prepares gel food.

Taking Care of the Tanks

Aquarists spend a lot of time taking care of the tanks in an aquarium. They go in the tanks two or three times a day to brush away **algae** and fish waste. The divers wear wetsuits to keep **bacteria** from their bodies out of the tanks.

The water in the tanks must be cleaned, too. It goes through huge **filters** that take out chemicals and bacteria that might harm the animals.

An aquarist cleans a tank with a water vacuum.▶

New Animals

Aquarists go out into the ocean to catch new sea animals. These new animals stay in special tanks for a few weeks to make sure they are not sick. Large fish like sharks may stay in a special pool in the back of the deep-sea tank. A gate keeps them apart from the other fish until they get used to each other. After a few weeks the aquarists lift the gate and let the new fish into the main tank with the other fish.

▲

An aquarist teaches the aquarium's new sea
turtle where to find food.

Did You Know?

- The first public aquarium opened in 1853 at the London Zoo in London, England. In 1859, the first aquarium in the United States opened. Called the Aquarial Gardens, it was in Boston, Massachusetts.

- The biggest aquarium in the world is the Georgia Aquarium in Atlanta. It has more than one million animals in tanks holding more than 8 million gallons (30 million liters) of water.

- Tank windows can be 3 to 13 inches (8 to 30 cm) thick. The windows are made of tough plastic.

- The National Aquarium in Baltimore, Maryland has more than one million visitors a year.

- If it seems dark inside an aquarium, that's because it is! Light is often kept low so that it's like the darkest parts of the ocean.

- Some aquariums have summer camps! You can go there and learn if you want to become a curator or educator when you grow up.

Glossary

algae (AL jee) — green, plant-like living things that grow in water and can coat glass and other objects in an aquarium

aquarist (aq KWARE ist) — person who is trained to take care of water animals

bacteria (back TEER ee uh) — tiny living things that can cause disease

coral reef (Kor el reef) — white, pink, or reddish stony structures in the ocean formed by the skeletons of millions of tiny sea animals

educator (EJ you kate r) — person at a museum, planetarium, or other public place who teaches people about the exhibits

filter (FILL tr) — device that uses chemicals, cloth, or other materials to clean water in aquarium tanks

scuba gear (SKOO bah GEER) — equipment that allows people to breathe underwater

technician (tek NISH in) — person who is specially trained to do a certain job

Index

Further Reading

Gorman, Jacqueline. *Aquarium*. Weekly Reader Early Learning Library, 2005.

Guest, Elissa. *Iris and Walter and the Field Trip*. Harcourt, 2007.

Websites to Visit

www.sheddaquarium.org

aquarium.ucsd.edu

www.neaq.org/scilearn/kids/

About the Author

Jennifer B. Gillis is an author and editor of nonfiction books and poetry for children. A graduate of Gilford College in North Carolina, she has taught foreign language and social studies in North Carolina, Virginia, and Illinois.